Rhythms
AND ROUTINES
A Parent's Guide to
Managing Life with Littles

BY NATASHA CABALLERO

Copyright ©2025 Natasha Caballero

Published by: Natasha Caballero LLC
Design by: Natasha Caballero
Canva Stock Images
Canva AI generated images

All rights reserved. No part of this book may be reproduced, distributed, or transmitted in any form or by any means, without the prior written permission of the publisher, except in the case of brief quotations embodied in critical reviews and certain other noncommercial uses permitted by copyright law.

This resource is designed to offer encouragement and support, especially for parents navigating the everyday joys and challenges of family life. The content reflects personal experience, creative ideas, and intentional tools meant to inspire reflection, not replace professional advice. Please use your discretion and adapt anything shared here to fit your unique season, values, and needs.

First Edition
ISBN 979-8-9929108-1-0

Dedication

To my family—your unwavering support means more to me than words can express. Through every high and low, you have been my greatest cheerleaders, and I am forever grateful.

Rhythms
AND ROUTINES
A Parent's Guide to Managing Life with Littles

BY NATASHA CABALLERO

Table of Contents

PG2   **INTRO**

PG6   **CHAPTER 1:**
            BUILD A STEADY RHYTHM

PG16   **CHAPTER 2:**
            PLAN WITH PURPOSE

PG28   **CHAPTER 3:**
            STREAMLINE WITH SYSTEMS

PG46   **CHAPTER 4:**
            FLEX & FLOW

PG54 CONCLUSION

PG56 RESOURCES

PG57 APPENDIX

PG64 ABOUT THE AUTHOR

"The days are long, but the years are short. Savor the small moments—they are the foundation of beautiful memories."

Intro

WHY?

Why do routines matter for young kids?

Routines are super important for young kids because they provide structure, security, and opportunities for learning. Here are a few key reasons why routines matter:

- **Emotional Security** – Knowing what to expect helps kids feel safe and reduces anxiety. Predictability makes the world feel more manageable.
- **Builds Independence** – When kids follow routines, they learn to do things on their own, like brushing their teeth or getting dressed.
- **Supports Learning & Development** – Consistent routines help with cognitive development, language skills, and problem-solving abilities by reinforcing repetition and practice.
- **Better Sleep & Eating Habits** – Having a set bedtime and mealtime routine helps regulate their body's internal clock, leading to better sleep and healthier eating habits.
- **Easier Transitions** – Kids struggle with sudden changes, but routines help prepare them for transitions, whether it's leaving for school or winding down for bed.

- **Encourages Positive Behavior** – Clear expectations help prevent meltdowns and tantrums since kids know what's coming next.
- **Strengthens Family Bonding** – Daily routines like reading before bed or eating together create moments for connection and communication.

When managing life with littles, it helps to establish routines that have a balance between structure and flexibility.

This book is written to be a guide for parents – providing some ways to create rhythms and routines that work for their schedule and family lifestyle.

"Routines bring rhythm, and rhythm brings peace. A little structure today makes for a lot of joy tomorrow."

BUILD A STEADY RHYTHM

Why Consistency Helps Kids Feel Secure

Children thrive on predictability because it creates a sense of safety. Knowing what to expect reduces anxiety and builds confidence.

Consistent routines provide:

1. Emotional Security – Reassures children that their needs will be met.

2. Behavioral Benefits – Minimizes power struggles and tantrums by setting clear expectations.

3. Cognitive Development – Familiar patterns free up mental energy for learning and creativity.

4. Stronger Parent-Child Connection – Daily rituals, like morning hugs or bedtime stories, build trust.

Routines vary based on a child's age and developmental stage. Here are examples of daily rhythms:

Infants (0-12 months)
• Morning: Wake up, feed, diaper change, tummy time or sensory play, nap.
• Midday: Feed, interactive play (songs, books), nap.
• Afternoon: Feed, outdoor time (stroller walk), quiet play, nap.
• Evening: Feed, bath, bedtime routine (massage, lullabies, dim lights).

Toddlers (1-3 years)
• Morning: Wake up, breakfast, independent play, structured activity (crafts, music), snack, outdoor play.
• Midday: Lunch, storytime, nap.
• Afternoon: Snack, sensory play, free play, dinner prep.
• Evening: Dinner, bath, bedtime routine (books, cuddles, lights out).

Preschoolers (3-5 years)
• Morning: Wake up, breakfast, get dressed, structured learning, snack, outdoor play.
• Midday: Lunch, rest time, creative play.
• Afternoon: Snack, social play, independent play, dinner prep.
• Evening: Dinner, bath, bedtime routine (reflection, gratitude, storytime).

Check out this time-block example on the next page.

TIME BLOCK EXAMPLE

AM

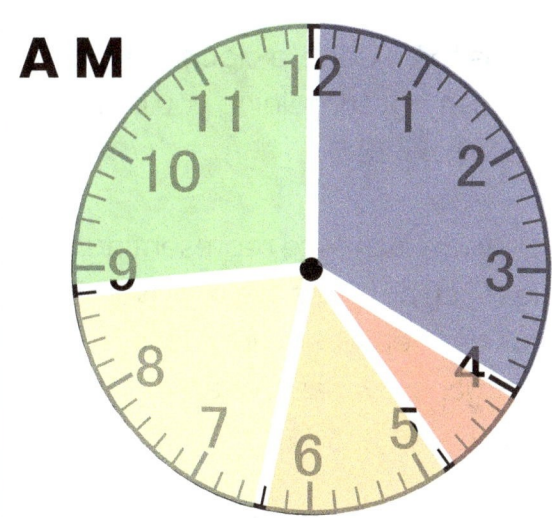

PM

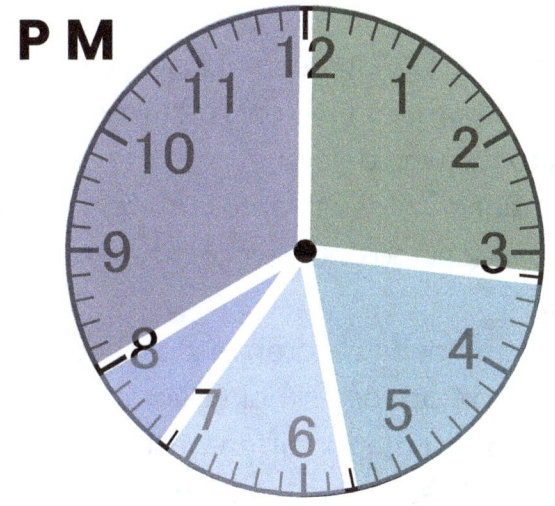

	Quiet Time
	Work out/ coffee
	Wake up routine
	Morning
	Midday
	Evening
	Dinner
	Bedtime routine
	Sleep

The Power of Using a Clock for Time Blocking

One of the most effective ways to visualize a full 24-hour day is by using a clock to create time blocks. While lists and schedules can outline what needs to be done, a clock offers a tangible way to see how time is distributed, helping you build a routine that feels balanced and achievable.

Think of your day as a pie chart, with each slice representing a specific time block for activities such as meals, naps, playtime, work, or rest. This method helps you see where your time is going at a glance and can reveal gaps, overlaps, or areas where adjustments are needed.

Using a clock for time blocking is especially helpful for:

- Understanding the flow of the day – Instead of just seeing a list of tasks, you can see how much time each activity actually takes in relation to the whole day.
- Creating realistic expectations – A visual representation helps ensure you're not overloading one part of the day while neglecting another.
- Helping kids grasp routines – Young children respond well to visual cues. A color-coded clock or a simple diagram can help them understand when it's time for different activities.
- Reducing decision fatigue – By assigning blocks of time for key tasks, you free yourself from having to constantly decide what to do next.

Overcoming Resistance to Routines

Even with well-planned routines, kids may resist structure. Here's how to navigate challenges:

1. Involve Them – Offer choices ("Do you want to brush teeth before or after pajamas?").

2. Use Visual Aids – Picture schedules or charts help younger kids anticipate what's next.

3. Make Transitions Fun – Use songs, timers, or games to ease activity changes.

4. Stay Flexible but Firm – Maintain consistency while adjusting to moods and circumstances.

5. Model the Routine – Kids follow routines more easily when they see parents doing the same.

6. Use Positive Reinforcement – Praise and small rewards (e.g., sticker charts) encourage participation.

You know yourself and your child best. So work with what serves you and your family best in your current season, and don't be afraid to switch things up if necessary.

CREATE YOUR TIMEBLOCKS

WEEKDAY VS. WEEKENDS

"You are not just raising children; you are shaping future hearts, minds, and souls. Give yourself grace in the process."

PLAN WITH PURPOSE

A structured routine shouldn't feel restrictive—it should create balance and ease. A well-planned rhythm allows flexibility while ensuring essential needs are met.

How to Create a Flexible Schedule Without Feeling Trapped

Worried about routines feeling too rigid? Here's how to keep them adaptable:

1. Focus on Anchors, Not Exact Times – Base routines on natural parts of the day (morning, afternoon, evening) rather than strict time slots. "Morning" one day can be 9-12, and 8:30-11:30 the next based on what activities you have planned later on that day.

2. Identify Non-Negotiables – Prioritize essentials like sleep, meals, and school, while keeping other activities flexible.

3. Use Time Blocks Instead of Hourly Plans

– Example:
  • Morning: Wake up, breakfast, play.
  • Midday: Lunch, quiet time, creative activities.
  • Afternoon: Outdoor play, snack, free play.
  • Evening: Dinner, bedtime routine, storytime.

4. Leave Room for Spontaneity – Be open to last-minute activities like an impromptu park trip.

5. Adapt to Energy Levels – Adjust based on whether your child needs active play or quiet time.

6. Give Yourself Grace – Some days won't go as planned, and that's okay.

Prioritizing Needs: Sleep, Meals, Learning, Play, Self-Care

A balanced routine supports both your child's well-being and your own.

• Sleep: Set consistent wake-up and bedtime routines; adjust naps based on age.

• Meals: Establish regular mealtimes and encourage healthy eating habits.

• Learning: Incorporate play-based learning; use daily moments (e.g., cooking, nature walks) as learning opportunities.

• Play: Mix independent play, guided play, and outdoor activities.

• Self-Care: Carve out time for yourself—whether it's morning coffee or a quiet moment after bedtime.

When starting out, start with one and build from there. It takes time to get used to something new for both you and your littles. After you take one step, you can grow into the next one.

OUR TOP 3 ESTABLISHED ROUTINES

Early on, we established 3 anchor routines specifically to help ground our day:

1. Morning Routine: starting each day fresh and clean
2. Bathtime Routine: placed strategically in the midday to serve as a reset & refresh as well as down time
3. Bedtime Routine: ending each day winding down with another refresh

All three involved the bathroom and the habits of hygiene, creating another way to teach by example and modeling.

Here is what this looked like for us:

Morning Routine

Change nappy
(use potty once trained)

Brush teeth

Get dressed

Bathtime Routine

Undress
(and place nappy/clothes in proper areas when developmentally capable)

Scrub/Shampoo
Conditioner/Rinse

Get dressed

Bedtime Routine

Go potty

Brush teeth

Change into PJ's
(and nappy if not trained)

Get in bed
(read a book)

Pray

WHAT ROUTINES DO YOU WANT TO ESTABLISH?

_____
_____
_____
_____
_____
_____
_____
_____
_____
_____
_____
_____
_____
_____
_____

"You were chosen to be their parent for a reason. Trust yourself, lean into love, and take it one moment at a time."

Chapter 3

STREAMLINE WITH SYSTEMS

Home systems, when implemented effectively, can benefit kids by fostering responsibility, organization, and a sense of security, ultimately leading to better academic performance and a smoother family life.

Encouraging Independence with Kid-Friendly Organization

Help kids take ownership of their routines with simple, accessible systems:

1. Simplify Choices – Rotate toys to prevent overwhelm; use easy-to-reach bins for clothing.

2. Label Everything – Use pictures or words on storage bins for non-readers.

3. Make Clean-Up Fun – Set a timer, use a cleanup song, or encourage a "one toy out at a time" rule.

4. Encourage Self-Sufficiency – Teach kids to pack their bags, dress themselves, and participate in daily tasks.

OUR TOP 3 ESTABLISHED SYSTEMS

Over the years, we've developed systems to bring order to what quickly became chaos as our family grew to five in just five years.

One of our top three systems is our "No-Fold" system.

1. The No-Fold Laundry System: A Game-Changer for Busy Parents

Laundry is one of those never-ending tasks that can quickly pile up—literally and figuratively. Folding clothes for multiple little ones? That's a time commitment I decided to ditch.

Instead, I use a No-Fold System, and it has been a game-changer for our home.

How It Works:

Rather than folding and neatly stacking tiny clothes that will inevitably be tossed around, I have designated bins for each child's clothing.

Once laundry is washed and dried, I simply sort the clean clothes into their assigned bins based on size and child—no folding required!

The Benefits of a No-Fold System:

- Laundry is done in a fraction of the time.

Folding takes time, but sorting into bins? Quick and painless. This method has drastically cut down the time I spend on laundry.

- It encourages a minimalist wardrobe.

With bins, I can easily see how many outfits each child has, helping me keep track of what they actually wear. It prevents excess and ensures that every piece of clothing has a purpose.

- Kids can dress themselves independently.

Since their clothes are sorted but not folded, little hands can grab what they need without messing up neatly stacked piles or mixing up their siblings' clothes. It fosters independence while keeping things organized.

- Clothes stay fresh and ready to wear.

Because we do laundry three times a week, nothing sits long enough to get overly wrinkled. The constant rotation ensures that everything is clean, accessible, and never buried at the bottom of a drawer.

This system is simple, stress-free, and perfect for busy parents who want to spend less time folding and more time living.

Number 2 of our top three systems is my "Tidy Time" system.

2. Tidy Time: The Simple System for Keeping the Chaos Under Control

Let's be real—kids and messes go hand in hand. But instead of waiting until the end of the day for a massive cleanup, I use a simple and effective system called Tidy Time to keep our home manageable throughout the day.

What is Tidy Time?

Unlike a traditional "clean-up" time where everything gets put back in its designated spot, Tidy Time is a quick reset that helps prevent overwhelming messes.

I have empty bins in every room where my kids play, specifically for this purpose. When I call out "Tidy Time," my kids know it's time to gather anything that's out and toss it into the bin—no sorting, no stress, just a simple, quick reset.

Why It Works (Even for Toddlers!)

This method is perfect for little ones, even as early as 18 months. At this stage—also known as the "dumping stage"—toddlers love the motion of picking things up and placing them in containers. Tidy Time turns that natural instinct into a helpful habit!

The Benefits of Tidy Time:

- Instant Relief from the Mess

Any time I start feeling overstimulated by clutter, I can call out "Tidy Time," and within minutes, the space is clear. No nagging, no stress—just a simple reset.

- Encourages Teamwork & Independence

The kids work together toward a common goal, making it feel like a game rather than a chore. Over time, they develop a sense of responsibility for their space.

- Builds the Habit of Cleaning Up

Tidy Time happens throughout the day, making it easier for kids to transition into Clean-Up Time later. Clean-Up Time is when we actually put things back where they belong and do deeper cleaning (like wiping down tables or vacuuming).

- Prepares Kids for a Lifetime of Organization

By keeping the home "tidy" throughout the day, my kids naturally develop the habit of maintaining an organized space, rather than letting the mess pile up.

This system has completely changed how we manage messes in our home. It's quick, effective, and—best of all—even toddlers can do it!

And number three of our top three systems (which happens to be my favorite) is called "The Costco".

3. The Costco System: A One-Trip Solution for Resetting Your Home

If you've ever been to Costco (or any big-box store), you've probably seen random items left in the wrong spots—an abandoned pack of muffins in the toy aisle or a case of water left at the checkout.

Instead of returning each item one by one, employees gather everything into a cart and then put it back in one efficient round trip.

I use this same principle in our home. Instead of running back and forth putting things away one at a time, I use what I call The Costco System to quickly reset our space.

How It Works

- Grab a Crate (or Basket):

I keep an instacrate handy, but any bin or basket will work. When I'm tidying up a room, I place anything that doesn't belong there into the crate.

- **Focus on One Room at a Time:**

Instead of getting distracted by putting items away in different rooms, I stay focused on fully resetting the space I'm in.

- **One-Trip Reset:**

Once I've finished clearing the room, I take my crate and, in one efficient trip, return everything to its proper place.

Why This Works So Well

- **Prevents Distraction**

Have you ever started cleaning the living room, picked up a stray coffee mug, and then found yourself unloading the entire dishwasher instead? This system keeps you focused on finishing one space before moving on.

- **Eliminates Back-and-Forth Trips**

Instead of wasting time and energy running to different rooms multiple times, you gather everything first and put it away in one round trip.

- **Works for the Whole Family**

This isn't just for kids—my husband and I also use this system to keep things from migrating all over the house.

- **Makes Cleaning Faster & More Efficient**

By decluttering a room first, I can actually clean it without distractions, making the entire process faster.

- The Most Efficient Way to Reset Your Home

The Costco System is a simple yet powerful way to tidy up without wasting time or getting sidetracked. It helps me stay focused, clears visual clutter quickly, and makes resetting the house a breeze.

WHAT SYSTEMS WOULD HELP YOU THE MOST?

_____
_____
_____
_____
_____
_____
_____
_____
_____
_____
_____
_____
_____
_____
_____

"Perfection is not the goal—presence is. Your children need you, not an idealized version of parenting."

Chapter 4

FLEX & FLOW

Life is unpredictable, and routines should support your family—not stress you out.

What to Do When Routines Get Disrupted

1. Prioritize Essentials – Focus on sleep, meals, connection, and rest.

2. Create Temporary Mini-Routines – Establish a simplified structure during major changes.

3. Use Transitional Cues – Maintain familiar bedtime steps even if the timing shifts.

4. Prepare Your Child – Explain changes in advance: "Today will be different because Grandma is visiting, but we'll still have storytime."

5. Make It Fun – Turn disruptions into adventures rather than stressors.

6. Ease Back Into Routine – Reintroduce structure gradually after a disruption.

Adjusting as Kids Grow

As children develop, routines should evolve:

• Recognize transitions (e.g., dropping naps, new school schedules).

• Give kids a say in routines to build independence.

• Adapt for life changes (e.g., new sibling, moving, school start).

Steps for the Parent

1. Let Go of Perfection – Some days won't go smoothly, and that's okay.

2. Lean on Your Village – Connect with other parents for support and encouragement.

3. Prioritize Your Well-Being – A rested, supported parent creates a calmer household.

Giving Yourself Grace: When the Plan Falls Apart

No matter how well you structure your day, life with little ones is unpredictable. Some days, everything flows smoothly. Other days, it feels like nothing goes according to plan—naps are skipped, tantrums are had, and meals take twice as long as they should.

Chapter 4

FLEX & FLOW

Life is unpredictable, and routines should support your family—not stress you out.

What to Do When Routines Get Disrupted

1. Prioritize Essentials – Focus on sleep, meals, connection, and rest.

2. Create Temporary Mini-Routines – Establish a simplified structure during major changes.

3. Use Transitional Cues – Maintain familiar bedtime steps even if the timing shifts.

4. Prepare Your Child – Explain changes in advance: "Today will be different because Grandma is visiting, but we'll still have storytime."

5. Make It Fun – Turn disruptions into adventures rather than stressors.

6. Ease Back Into Routine – Reintroduce structure gradually after a disruption.

Adjusting as Kids Grow

As children develop, routines should evolve:

• Recognize transitions (e.g., dropping naps, new school schedules).

• Give kids a say in routines to build independence.

• Adapt for life changes (e.g., new sibling, moving, school start).

Steps for the Parent

1. Let Go of Perfection – Some days won't go smoothly, and that's okay.

2. Lean on Your Village – Connect with other parents for support and encouragement.

3. Prioritize Your Well-Being – A rested, supported parent creates a calmer household.

Giving Yourself Grace: When the Plan Falls Apart

No matter how well you structure your day, life with little ones is unpredictable. Some days, everything flows smoothly. Other days, it feels like nothing goes according to plan—naps are skipped, tantrums are had, and meals take twice as long as they should.

But here's the truth: **flexibility isn't failure.**

When schedules unravel, it's easy to feel frustrated or defeated. That's why learning to extend grace to yourself and your family is just as important as having a plan in the first place.

Ways to Give Yourself Grace When the Day Falls Apart

- Remember That Routines Are Tools, Not Chains

Your schedule is meant to serve your family, not the other way around. If something isn't working one day, it doesn't mean the routine is broken—it just means life happened.

- Focus on the Big Picture

Instead of getting stuck on what didn't happen, ask:

  - Did my kids feel loved today?
  - Did we have some connection, even in the chaos?
  - Is tomorrow a new opportunity to reset?

If the answers are yes, then the day was still a win.

- Have a "Reset Button"

When things start spiraling, take a moment to pause and reset. That might mean:

  - Taking 5 deep breaths.
  - Turning on calming music.
  - Stepping outside for a quick change of scenery.
  - Calling a "Tidy Time" or a snack break to shift the energy.

A small reset can make a big difference in salvaging a rough day.

- Lean on Simple Wins

When the schedule falls apart, focus on small victories:

  - Read a book together.
  - Get outside for fresh air.
  - Have a "yes moment" where you set aside the to-do list and just enjoy your kids for a few minutes.

Some days, the best rhythm is just showing up and trying again tomorrow.

- Give Yourself the Same Kindness You'd Give a Friend

If your best friend told you her day was a disaster, you wouldn't shame her—you'd reassure her. Talk to yourself with that same kindness. You are doing your best, and that is enough.

BE KIND
to yourself

"Messy days and tired nights may feel endless, but love is the legacy you're building with every hug, every meal, and every bedtime story."

Conclusion

Encouragement for Parents: You're Doing Better Than You Think

Some days, the routine flows effortlessly. Other days, it's chaos. But here's the truth: It's not about perfection—it's about presence.

Your child won't remember if every routine was perfectly followed. They'll remember feeling safe, loved, and valued. On tough days, remind yourself:

- ✓ You are showing up.
- ✓ You are loving your child the best way you can.
- ✓ You are learning and growing together.

Give yourself grace. The best memories often come from unplanned moments—the extra cuddle, the spontaneous dance party, the belly laughs at dinner.

At the end of the day, connection matters more than perfection.

You're doing better than you think!

Resources

To help you implement the rhythms and routines in this book, I've created a collection of digital downloads you can access anytime.

These resources are designed to simplify your daily life, giving you flexible tools to create a system that works for your family.

Visit my website to download and print them!

 **Access all printable resources here:**
natashacaballero.com

Join the Community! @_caballerocollaborations

Appendix

Appendix Disclaimer:
The following sections provide examples of how routines and schedules can be adapted for different parenting situations. However, every family is unique, and these categories only represent a few of the many ways parents navigate daily life with little ones.

If your experience isn't reflected here, please know that your story matters. I'd love to hear how you create routines that work for your family! Feel free to share your insights and experiences with me at natashaluannacaballero@gmail.com or connect on Instagram @_caballerocollaborations—we grow stronger together.

Appendix: Adapting Routines for Different Parenting Styles

Every family's situation is unique, and routines should be adaptable to fit different lifestyles and needs. Below are some tailored strategies for various parenting styles:

1. Working Parents
Balancing work responsibilities with parenting can be challenging, but routines can help create smoother transitions and quality family time.

• Balancing childcare, work hours, and family time – Plan key moments for connection, such as breakfast together, post-work check-ins, or bedtime routines.

• Preparing routines that work for daycare, school, or caregivers – Create a consistent drop-off and pick-up routine to ease transitions and provide kids with a sense of security.

• Time-saving tips for mornings and evenings – Prep lunches, backpacks, and clothes the night before to minimize morning stress. Use a shared family calendar for scheduling.

2. Stay-at-Home Parents

Having structure at home can prevent burnout and keep kids engaged while allowing flexibility for daily life.

• Creating structure without feeling stuck in a rigid schedule – Use "anchor points" in the day (meals, naps, outdoor time) to maintain consistency without needing strict timing.

• Keeping kids engaged while managing household responsibilities – Rotate independent play, structured activities, and outdoor time to balance stimulation and free play.

• Finding time for self-care and social connections – Schedule breaks, playdates, or personal time (even short moments for reading or coffee) to recharge.

3. Work-from-Home Parents

Juggling remote work and parenting requires a thoughtful approach to routines.

• Managing kids while working remotely – Set up independent activity stations for kids to engage with while you work. Use designated quiet times for focused tasks.

• Setting realistic expectations for productivity – Prioritize work tasks based on your child's schedule (e.g., deep work during naps, lighter tasks while they play).

• Creating a family-friendly workspace and schedule – Use visual schedules to show kids when you're available and when they need to play independently.

4. Homeschooling Parents

Homeschooling allows flexibility but benefits from a structured rhythm.

• Blending learning into daily routines – Incorporate educational moments into everyday tasks (cooking = math, nature walks = science).

• Establishing a school-day flow that works for different ages – Use short learning blocks with breaks in between, and allow hands-on or interest-based learning.

• Keeping flexibility while maintaining consistency – Stick to key learning times but allow for spontaneous field trips, outdoor exploration, or creative projects.

5. Single Parents

Managing everything solo means routines should be streamlined and stress-reducing.

• Simplifying routines to reduce stress – Focus on essentials like meals, sleep, and connection rather than trying to structure every part of the day.

• Maximizing support systems and resources – Use meal planning, shared childcare (if possible), or community resources to lighten the load.

• Finding balance between structure and spontaneity – Create predictability but allow room for flexibility when needed.

6. Parents of Neurodivergent Kids

Children with sensory, emotional, or developmental differences may need extra support with transitions and structure.

• Adapting routines to meet sensory and emotional needs – Offer quiet time, weighted blankets, or movement breaks to regulate sensory input.

• Using visual supports, timers, and transition strategies – Picture schedules, countdown timers, and advance warnings can help ease changes in routine.

• Allowing flexibility while maintaining predictability – Keep core parts of the routine stable (e.g., bedtime, meals) while adjusting activities based on their energy and focus levels.

By recognizing that different parenting styles require different approaches, you can create a routine that works best for your family's unique dynamics while maintaining a balance of structure and flexibility.

About the Author

Natasha Caballero is a writer, speaker, and creative entrepreneur passionate about helping parents navigate life with young children. As a homeschooling mom of three boys under six, she understands the challenges and joys of creating routines that work for busy families.

She is the founder of Natasha Caballero LLC, a creative hub specializing in music lessons, photography, event planning, and customized products designed to bring joy and convenience to families. She is also the author of Let's Get Curious and has shared her insights through talks such as Turning to Jesus in the Mundane.

Through her work, Natasha strives to encourage and equip parents with practical tools, creative ideas, and heartfelt connection.

To connect, reach out via email at natashaluannacaballero@gmail.com or follow along on Instagram @_caballerocollaborations

FIND MORE ONLINE AT NATASHACABALLERO.COM

She is | Proverbs 31 by Natasha Caballero

| She is: FAITHFUL | $28.99 | She is: FAITHFUL | $24.99 | She is: FAITHFUL | $29.99 | She is: FAITHFUL | $19.99 |

Portfolio

More

About

Our Story

Natasha Caballero LLC is a creative hub founded by a passionate stay-at-home mom. We specialize in music lessons, photography, event planning/decor, and customized products/planning and ideas for parents of young children.

Our mission is to provide exceptional services that add joy and convenience to the lives of parents. With a commitment to quality and creativity, we strive to make every moment special for you and your family.

Learn More